Table Of Contents

AF726970

KINDERGARTEN

FIRST GRADE

Table Of Contents

SECOND GRADE

THIRD GRADE

Common Core State Standards for Reading Literature

KINDERGARTEN

Key Ideas and Details:

1.With prompting and support, ask and answer questions about key details in text.
2.With prompting and support, retell familiar stories, including key details.
3.With prompting and support, identify characters, settings, and major events in a story.

Craft and Structure:

4.Ask and answer questions about unknown words in text.
5.Recognize common types of texts (e.g., storybooks, poems).
6.With prompting and support, name the author and illustrator of a story and define the role of each in telling the story.

Integration of Knowledge and Ideas:

7.With prompting and support, describe the relationship between illustrations and the story in which they appear (e.g., what moment in a story an illustration depicts).
8.(Not applicable to literature).
9.With prompting and support, compare and contrast the adventures and experiences of characters in familiar stories.
10.Actively engage in group reading activities with purpose and understanding.

FIRST GRADE

Key Ideas and Details:

1.Ask and answer questions about key details in a text.
2.Retell stories, including key details, and demonstration understanding of their central message or lesson.
3.Describe characters, settings, and major events in a story, using key details.

Craft and Structure:

4.Identify words and phrases in stories or poems that suggest feelings or appeal to the senses.
5.Explain major differences between books that tell stories and books that give information, drawing on a wide reading of a range of text types.
6.Identify who is telling the story at various points in a text.

Integration of Knowledge and Ideas:

7.Use illustrations and details in a story to describe its characters, setting, or events.
8.(Not applicable to literature).
9.Compare and contrast the adventures and experiences of characters in stories.

Range of Reading and Level of Text Complexity:

10.With prompting and support, read prose and poetry of appropriate complexity for grade 1.

SECOND GRADE

Key Ideas and Details:

1.Ask and answer such questions as who, what, where, when, why, and how to demonstrate understanding of key details in a text.
2.Recount stories, including fables and folktales from diverse cultures, and determine their central message, lesson, or moral.
3.Describe how characters in a story respond to major events and challenges.

Craft and Structure:

4.Describe how words and phrases (e.g., regular beats, alliteration, rhymes, repeated lines) supply rhythm and meaning in a story, poem, or song.
5.Describe the overall structure of a story, including describing how the beginning introduces the story and the ending concludes the action.
6.Acknowledge differences in the points of view of characters, including by speaking in a different voice for each character when reading dialogue aloud.

Integration of Knowledge and Ideas:

7.Use information gained from the illustrations and words in a print or digital text to demonstrate understanding of its characters, setting, or plot.
8.(Not applicable to literature).
9.Compare and contrast two or more versions of the same story (e.g., Cinderella stories) by different authors or from different cultures.

Range of Reading and Level of Text Complexity:

10.By the end of the year, read and comprehend literature, including stories and poetry, in the grades 2-3 text complexity band proficiently, with scaffolding as needed at the high end of the range.

THIRD GRADE

Key Ideas and Details:

1.Ask and answer questions to demonstrate understanding of a text, referring explicitly to the text as the basis for the answers.
2.Recount stories, including fables, folktales, and myths from diverse cultures; determine the central message, lesson, or moral and explain how it is conveyed through key details in the text.
3.Describe characters in a story (e.g., their traits, motivations, or feelings) and explain how their actions contribute to the sequence of events.

Craft and Structure:

4.Determine the meaning of words and phrases as they are used in a text, distinguishing literal from nonliteral language.
5.Refer to parts of stories, dramas, and poems when writing or speaking about a text, using terms such as chapter, scene, and stanza; describe how each successive part builds on earlier sections.
6.Distinguish their own point of view from that of the narrator or those of the characters.

Integration of Knowledge and Ideas:

7.Explain how specific aspects of a text's illustrations contribute to what is conveyed by the words in a story (e.g., create mood, emphasize aspects of a character or setting).
8.(Not applicable to literature).
9.Compare and contrast the themes, settings, and plots of stories written by the same author about the same or similar characters (e.g., in books from a series).

Range of Reading and Level of Text Complexity:

10.By the end of the year, read and comprehend literature, including stories, dramas, and poetry, at the high end of the grades 2-3 text complexity band independently and proficiently.

Kindergarten Reading : Literature

LEVELS 2 LEARNING

Name: ______________ Date: ______________

Directions: Read about the bowls. Then write the answers.

Some  are big.

Some  are medium.

Some  are small.

1. How many bowls does the story tell about ?

2. Name the sizes of the bowls ?

3. What size bowl would you use ?

LEVELS 2 LEARNING

Name: ______________ Date: ______________

Directions: In each of the four sections, place a 1 for the event that comes first, a 2 for the event that comes second, and a 3 for the event that comes last.

1.

______Orsa sat in a chair.

______Orsa ate cereal.

______Orsa laid in a bed.

2.

______The Three Brothers made their beds.

______The Three brothers rode their bikes.

______The Three brothers sat at the table.

3.

______Orsa ate from the small bowl.

______Orsa ate from the big bowl.

______Orsa ate from the medium-sized bowl.

4.

______The little brother found Orsa.

______The little brother rode his bike.

______The little brother sat in his chair.

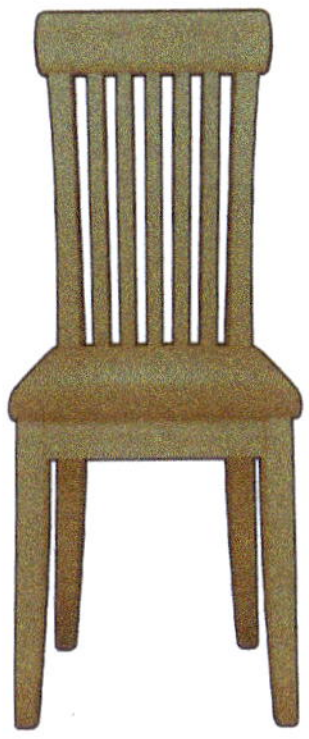

Name: ____________ Date: ____________

What can you recall ?

1. What color is Orsa's dress?

2. What room were the bowls in?

3. What was the house near?

4. What happened at the end of the story?

Name: ______________ Date: ______________

Directions: Choose a word you just learned and draw a picture to show what the word means.

I just learned the new word:

And it means:

Name: ____________ Date: ____________

Fiction Books are stories that are not real.

Non-Fiction Books are about real things.

Book covers help us determine and sort fiction and non-fiction books.

A Cut and sort the books in the appropriate columns.

Cut and sort the fiction books here:		

Cut and sort the non-fiction books here:		

B Draw the cover page of your favorite fiction and non-fiction book.

Name: ______________ Date: ______________

Directions: Cut out the labels below. Place them in the correct spaces to label the parts of the book.

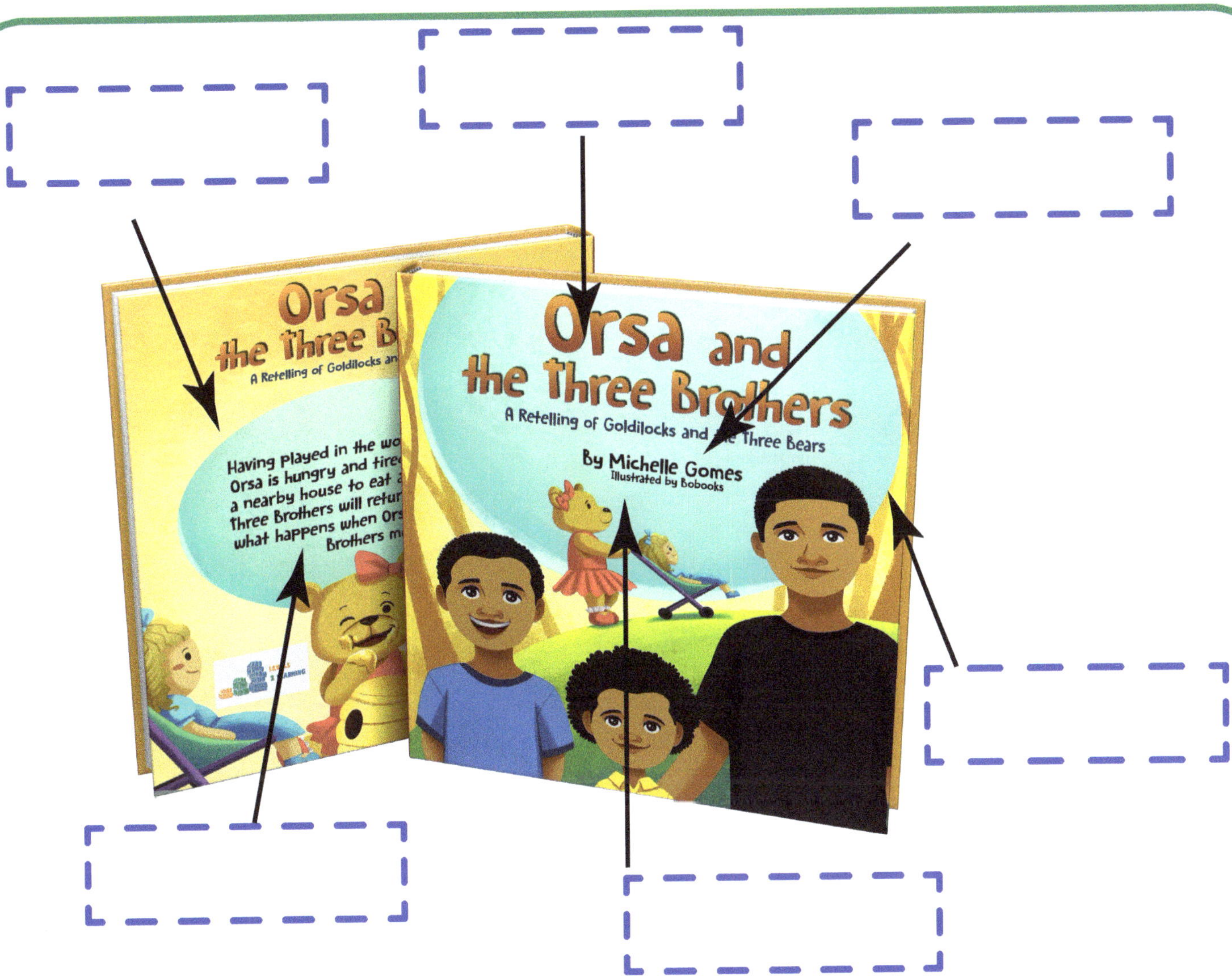

front cover	title	author
illustrator	summary	back cover

Name: ______________ Date: ______________

Directions: Look at the picture below. Answer the question using the picture.

Name: ______________ Date: ______________

Which sentence describes one (1) thing you see in the picture.

1) Big brother is wearing orange shorts.
2) There is oatmeal on the chairs.
3) The boys are happy.

Name: ______________ Date: ______________

What is the same and what is different ?

3 brothers

3 bears

LEVELS 2 LEARNING

Name: ____________ Date: ____________

Directions: Observe the pictures and answer the questions.

Name: ____________ Date: ____________

Directions: Observe the pictures and answer the questions.

1. Whose bed is Orsa in?	a. Big Brother b. Middle Brother c. Little Brother
2. What does Little brother do when he finds Orsa?	a. Screams b. Talk c. Cries
3. What color is Big brothers blanket?	a. Black b. Blue c. Pink
4. How many pillows are on Middle brothers bed?	a. 1 b. 2 c. 3

First Grade Reading : Literature

LEVELS
2 LEARNING

Name: ____________ Date: ____________

Directions: Read each statement below. Circle true or false.

1) This story is about a bear and three brothers. true false

2) Orsa has a stuffed turtle in her stroller. true false

3) Little brother makes the oatmeal. true false

4) Orsa eats out of a beehive. true false

5) Middle brothers bowl is medium-sized. true false

6) The house is by a pool. true false

Name: ______________ Date: ______________

What's the lesson?

1. Story title:

2. The lesson of the story was:

3. I know because:

Name: ______________ Date: ______________

Story Map

Book Title:

The Main Characters:

The Setting:

Beginning	Middle	End

Name: ____________ Date: ____________

Directions: Draw lines to match the words with their meanings.

1. Shout	• Unhappy.
2. Upset	• A loud call or cry.

Instructions: In this story the Three Brothers love to bike ride. Draw a picture of something that you love to do.

Name: ____________ Date: ____________

Directions: Read and answer the questions below.

1) The story of Orsa and the Three Brothers is:

a.Fiction b.Non-Fiction

2) How do you know?

____

Draw a picture from the story that is reality?	Draw a picture from the story that is not reality?

Name: ____________ Date: ____________

Directions: Read the sentence in each box. Then, circle the picture of the person speaking.

1) " Mm, something smells tasty "

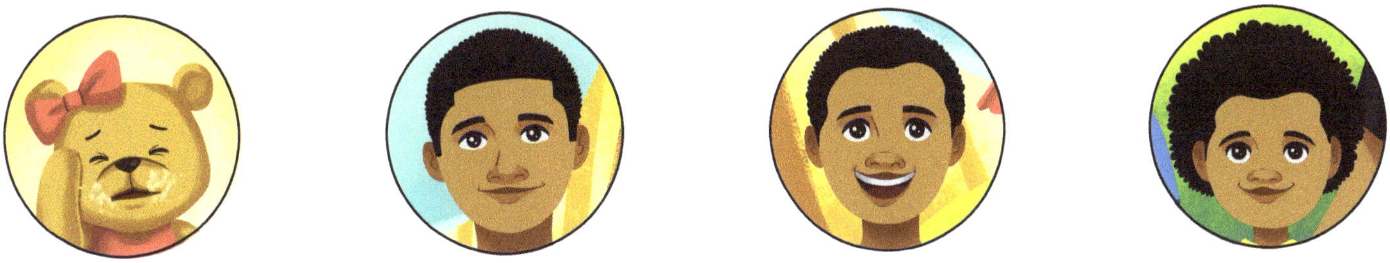

2) " And someone's still laying in mine! "

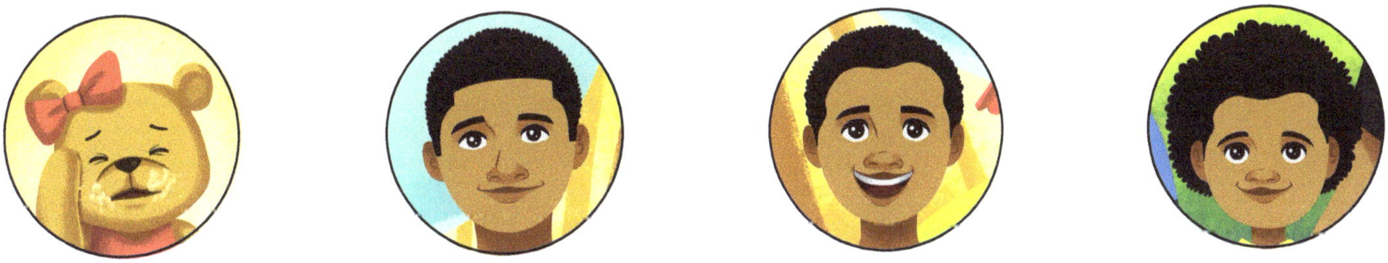

3) "Why did you make the oatmeal so hot? "

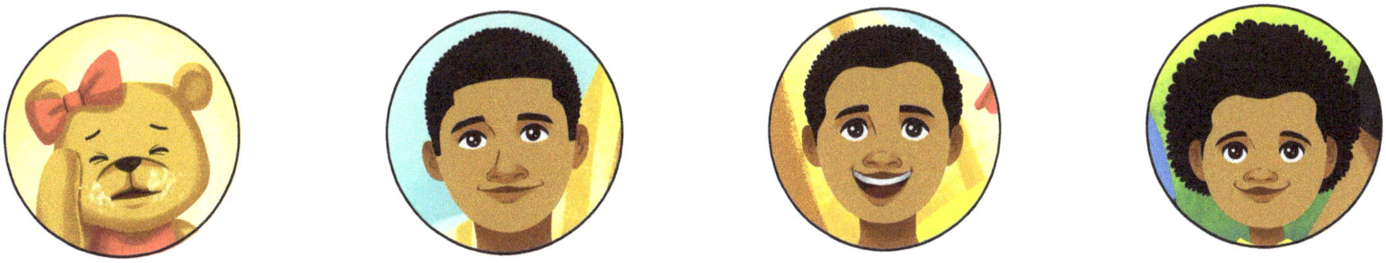

Name: ____________ Date: ____________

Directions: Use the illustrations to describe what is happening in each picture Color in the bubble next to the correct answer.

- ◯ The boys are jumping.
- ◯ The boys are sleeping.
- ◯ The boys are riding bikes.

- ◯ Orsa is running.
- ◯ Orsa is skipping .
- ◯ Orsa is walking.

- ◯ Orsa is eating from a beehive.
- ◯ Orsa is drinking juice.
- ◯ Orsa is clapping.

Name: ______________ Date: ______________

Directions: Read your favorite story. Then fill out the chart below as you think about how it is the same and different from Orsa and the Three Brothers.

	Story 1: Orsa and the Three Brothers	Story 2:
What happened?		
Who were the characters?		
Whose point of view was the story told from?		
Where did the story take place?		

Name: ____________ Date: ____________

Directions: Answer the question below about the characters feelings throughou[t] the story.

1. How do the Three brothers feel about each other ?

Second Grade Reading : Literature

LEVELS 2 LEARNING

Name: ____________ Date: ____________

Pick a Scene

Directions: Pick a scene in the book. Answer "Who" "What" "Where" "When" and "Why" about the scene.

Who

What

Where

When

Why

LEVELS 2 LEARNING

Name: ____________ Date: ____________

In your own words, write what this story is about.

____

____

____

____

What did the three brothers learn?

____

____

____

____

Name: ____________ Date: ____________

1. Write about a problem the three brothers have in the story, then write the solution.

Problem → Solution

2. How would you have solved the problem?

Name: ____________ Date: ____________

1. Circle the words in the sentence below that have one syllable/beat.

Before the Three Brothers had
a chance to say anything,
Orsa jumped up from
the bed,ran out the
door and into the woods.

2. Write four action words, with one syllable, to describe your favorite activity.

____

____

____

____

LEVELS 2 LEARNING

Name: ____________ Date: ____________

Fill in the details of the problem and story ending.

Problem

Who tried to solve the problem?	How did they try to solve it?	Solution: How did the story end?

Did you like the ending? Why or why not?

____

____

Name: ______________ Date: ______________

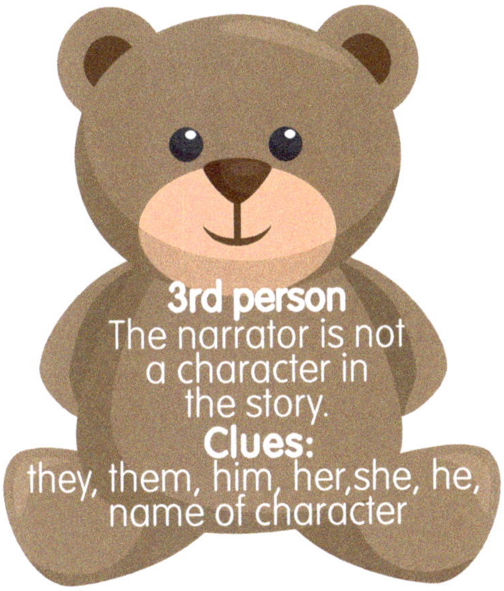

Directions: For each sentence decide if the sentence is in 1st, 2nd, or 3rd person, then circle the correct answer.

1) Every Saturday morning, in a house by the lake.	1st	2nd	3rd
2) Why did you make the oatmeal so hot?	1st	2nd	3rd
3) Yum, just right.	1st	2nd	3rd
4) Someone's been sitting in my chair.	1st	2nd	3rd

LEVELS 2 LEARNING

Name: ______________ Date: ______________

Directions: Write 3 sentences about your weekend in 2nd person.

2nd Person:

Name: ______________ Date: ______________

Directions: Look at the illustration and answer the following questions.

Name: ____________ Date: ____________

1. What does the illustration show ?

a. The three brothers are happy.

b. the three brothers are angry.

c. the three brothers are afraid.

2. What is the importance of this illustration to the story?

____

____

Name: ____________ Date: ____________

Directions: Compare "Orsa and the Three Brothers" to a version of "Goldilocks and the Three Bears" of your choice.

Orsa and the Three Brothers	Goldilocks and the Three Bears
Main Characters:	
Setting:	
Problem:	
Solution:	

Name: ____________ Date: ____________

Clues and Predictions

Directions: Predict what the three brothers will do the next time they leave their house to go for a bike ride.

Predict: "to say or estimate that (a specific thing) will happen in the future".

Clue: "Something that helps a person find something, understand something, or solve a mystery or a puzzle.

What do you predict?

____

____

Write a sentence from the book that gives a clue to support your prediction.

____

____

____

Third Grade Reading : Literature

Name: ____________ Date: ____________

Directions: Answer the following question by going back into the book.

1. What does Orsa eat? Support your answer with evidence from the text.

____

____

____

2. Do the Three brothers like to spend time together? Support your answer with evidence from the text.

____

____

____

____

Name: ______________ Date: ______________

3. Do the Three brothers share a room or have separate rooms? Support your answer with evidence from the text.

4. What did Orsa do at the end of the story? Support your answer with evidence from the text.

Name: ___________ Date: ___________

Directions: Answer the following question by going back into the book.

1. Why did the Three Brothers go for a bike ride?

2. How did Older brother respond when Middle Brother said his oatmeal was too hot?

3. What is the lesson in the story?

LEVELS 2 LEARNING

Name: ____________ Date: ____________

Directions: Choose a character from the story . Fill out the outlying boxes with information about that character.

What does the character talk about?

How do I feel about the character?

How does the character look?

What do others say about the character?

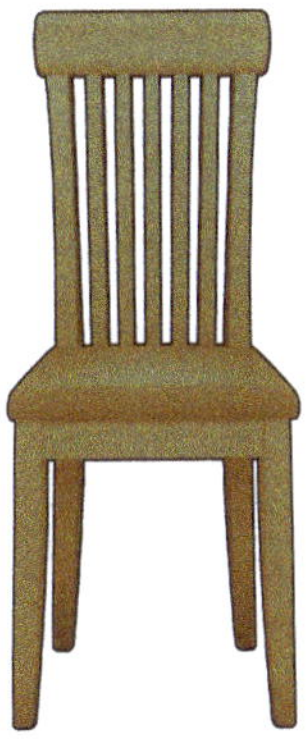

Name: ____________ Date: ____________

Word Web

Directions: Write a new word from the story in the center of the word web and fill in the boxes.

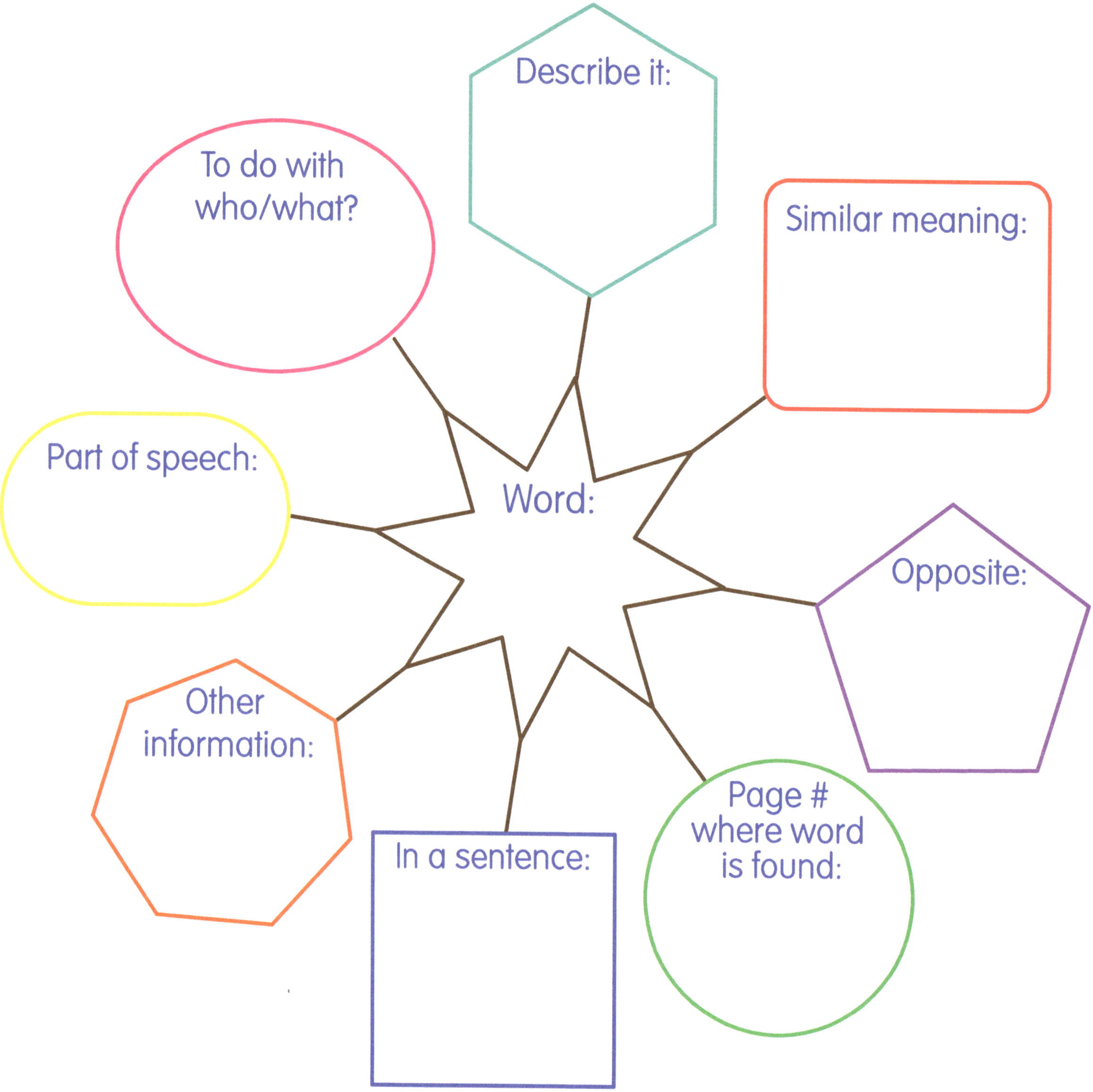

Name: ____________ Date: ____________

Beginning of story: ____________

____

Middle of story: ____________

____

How does the middle build on the beginning? ____________

____

____

End of story: ____________

____

How does the end build on the middle? ____________

____

____

Name: ____________ Date: ____________

Directions: Think about how something or someone in the story tha relates to you or someone else you know. Then answer the questions below.

Describe how something or someone in the story relates to you or someone you know.

____

____

____

____

How does your relating to the story, or the story's characters, help your understanding of the story?

____

____

____

____

LEVELS 2 LEARNING

Name: ____________ Date: ____________

Draw a character from the book

Directions: Write words that describe your character.

Name: ______________ Date: ______________

Directions: Choose two characters from the story. In the boxes below write their similarities and their differences. Pick the character you'd like to spend time with and explain why you chose them.

Character 1	Character 2
Similarities	**Differences**

Character you'd like to spend time with and why you chose them.

Name: ____________ Date: ____________

1. How did the story end?

2. Do you like the ending? Why? or Why Not?

3. Create your own ending to this story.

ANSWER KEY

LEVELS 2 LEARNING

Directions: Read about the bowls. Then write the answers.

Some  are big.

Some  are medium.

Some  are small.

---

1. How many bowls does the story tell about ?

The story tells about three bowls.

2. Name the sizes of the bowls ?

Big Medium Small

3. What size bowl would you use ?

Answers will vary.

Directions: In each of the four sections, place a 1 for the event that comes first, a 2 for the event that comes second, and a 3 for the event that comes last.

1.

__2__ Orsa sat in a chair.

__1__ Orsa ate cereal.

__3__ Orsa laid in a bed.

2.

__1__ The Three Brothers made their beds.

__3__ The Three brothers rode their bikes.

__2__ The Three brothers sat at the table.

3.

__3__ Orsa ate from the small bowl.

__1__ Orsa ate from the big bowl.

__2__ Orsa ate from the medium-sized bowl.

4.

__3__ The little brother found Orsa.

__2__ The little brother rode his bike.

__1__ The little brother sat in his chair.

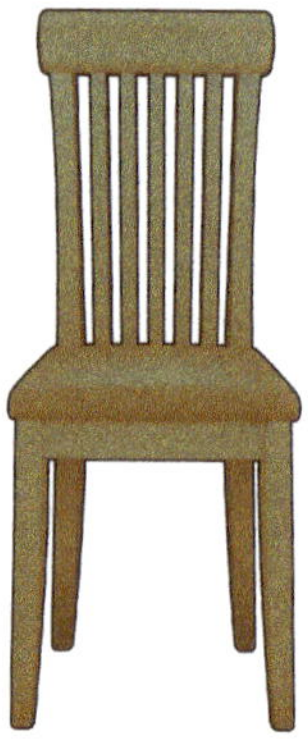

What can you recall ?

1. What color is Orsa's dress?

Pink.

2. What room were the bowls in?

The kitchen.

3. What was the house near?

A lake.

4. What happened at the end of the story?

Answers will vary.

A Cut and sort the books in the appropriate columns.

Cut and sort the fiction books here:

Cut and sort the non-fiction books here:

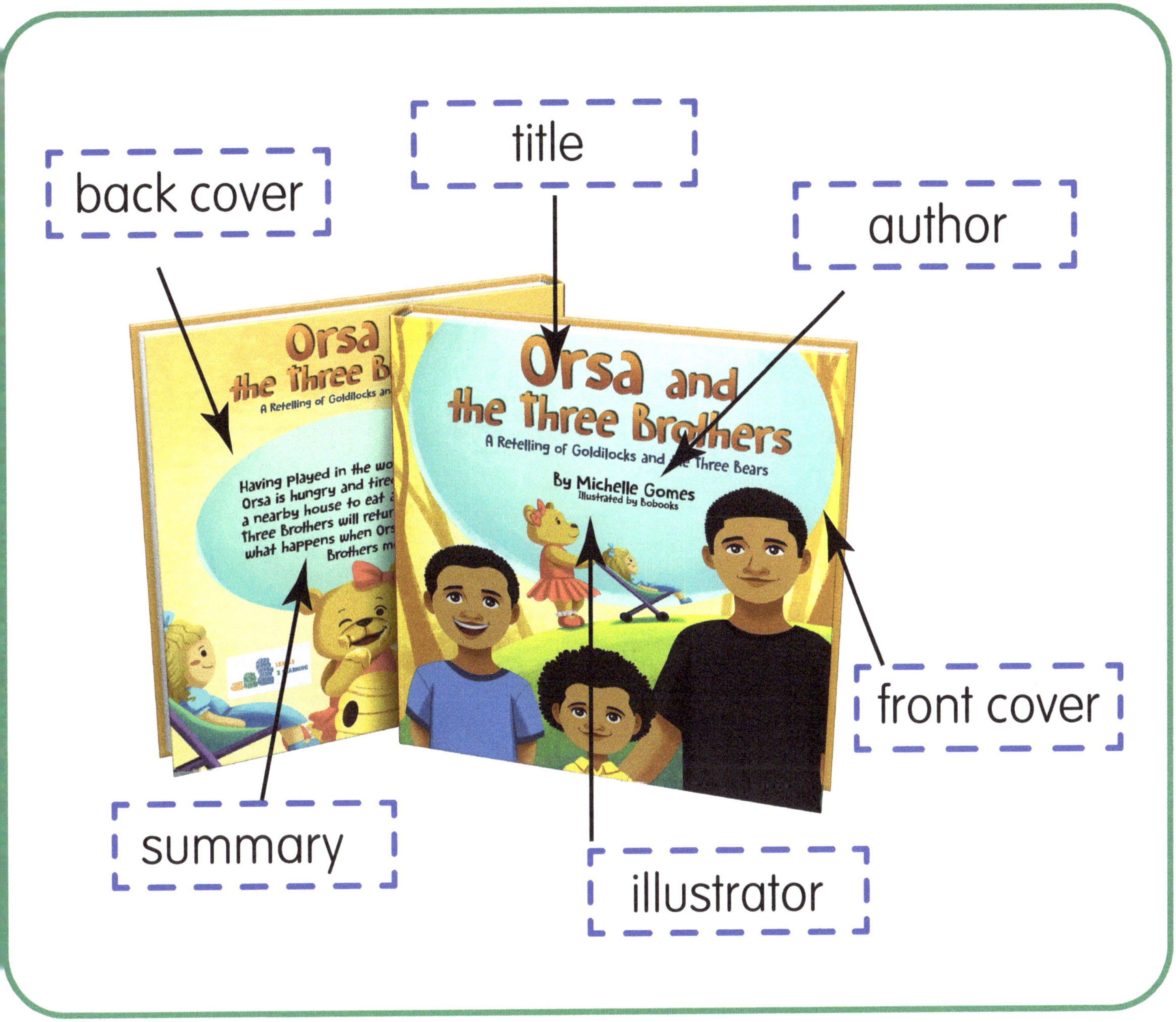

Author: a person who writes books, stories, plays, or other works.

Illustrator: an artist who makes illustrations for books or other written works.

Title: name of something such as a book, movie, or piece of music.

Which sentence describes one (1) thing you see in the picture.

1) Big brother is wearing orange shorts.
2) There is oatmeal on the chairs.
3) The boys are happy.

Directions: Observe the pictures and answer the questions.

1. Whose bed is Orsa in?	a. Big Brother b. Middle Brother (c.) Little Brother
2. What does Little brother do when he finds Orsa?	(a.) Screams b. Talk c. Cries
3. What color is Big brothers blanket?	a. Black (b.) Blue c. Pink
4. How many pillows are on Middle brothers bed?	a. 1 (b.) 2 c. 3

Directions: Read each statement below. Circle true or false.

1) This story is about a bear and three brothers.	true (circled)	false
2) Orsa has a stuffed turtle in her stroller.	true	false (circled)
3) Little brother makes the oatmeal.	true	false (circled)
4) Orsa eats out of a beehive.	true (circled)	false
5) Middle brothers bowl is medium-sized.	true (circled)	false
6) The house is by a pool.	true	false (circled)

What's the lesson?

1. Story title:

Orsa and the Three Brothers.

2. The lesson of the story was:

Answers may vary.

3. I know because:

Answers may vary.

Story Map

Book Title:

Orsa and the Three Brothers.

The Main Characters:

Orsa and the Three Brothers.

The Setting:

House in the woods.

Beginning	Middle	End
Answers may vary.	Answers may vary.	Answers may vary.

Directions: Draw lines to match the words with their meanings.

1. Shout	Unhappy.
2. Upset	A loud call or cry.

Directions: Read and answer the questions below.

1) The story of Orsa and the Three Brothers is:

(a.) Fiction b. Non-Fiction

2) How do you know?

Answers may vary.

Directions: Read the sentence in each box. Then, circle the picture of the person speaking.

1) " Mm, something smells tasty "

2) " And someone's still laying in mine! "

3) "Why did you make the oatmeal so hot? "

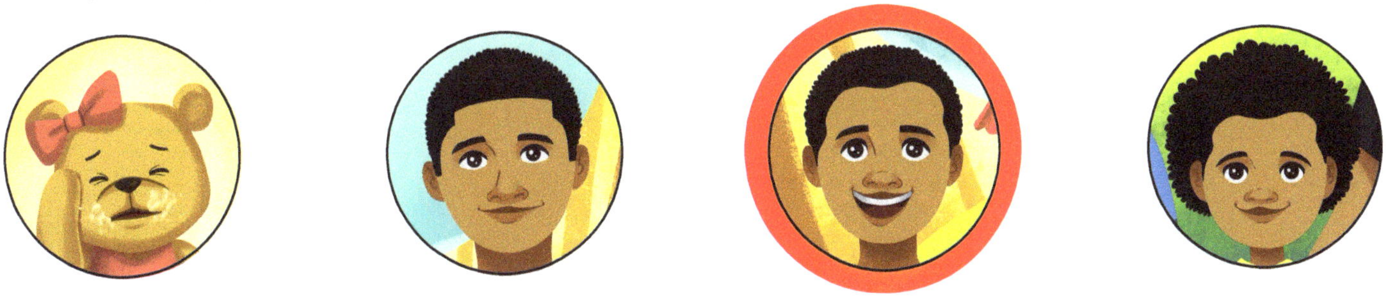

Directions: Use the illustrations to describe what is happening in each picture. Color in the bubble next to the correct answer.

- ○ The boys are jumping.
- ○ The boys are sleeping.
- ● The boys are riding bikes.

- ○ Orsa is running.
- ○ Orsa is skipping .
- ● Orsa is walking.

- ● Orsa is eating from a beehive.
- ○ Orsa is drinking juice.
- ○ Orsa is clapping.

In your own words, write what this story is about.

This story is about a bear named Orsa that goes into a strangers home and uses their things without permission.

What lesson did Gingerlocks learn?

The three brothers learned to always lock their door when they leave home.

1. Write about a problem the three brothers have in the story, then write the solution.

Problem

Answer will vary.

→

Solution

Answer will vary.

2. How would you have solved the problem?

Answers will vary.

1. Circle the words in the sentence below that have one syllable/beat.

Before the Three Brothers had
a chance to say anything,
Orsa jumped up from
the bed, ran out the
door and into the woods.

2. Write four action words, with one syllable, to describe your favorite activity.

Answers will vary.

Fill in the details of the problem and story ending.

Problem
Answers will vary.

Who tried to solve the problem?	How did they try to solve it?	Solution: How did the story end?
Answers will vary.	Answers will vary.	Answers will vary.

Did you like the ending? Why or why not?

Answers will vary.

Directions: For each sentence decide if the sentence is in 1st, 2nd, or 3rd person, then circle the correct answer.

1) Every Saturday morning, in a house by the lake.	1st	**2nd**	3rd
2) Why did you make the oatmeal so hot?	**1st**	2nd	3rd
3) Yum, just right.	**1st**	2nd	3rd
4) Someone's been sitting in my chair.	**1st**	2nd	3rd

1. What does the illustration show ?

(a.) The three brothers are happy.

b. the three brothers are angry.

c. the three brothers are afraid.

2. What is the importance of this illustration to the story?

The importance of this illustration is that it shows the three brothers solving their problem together.

Directions: Answer the following question by going back into the book.

1. What does Orsa eat? Support your answer with evidence from the text.

Answers will vary.

2. Do the Three brothers like to spend time together? Support your answer with evidence from the text.

Answers will vary.

3. Do the Three brothers share a room or have separate rooms? Support your answer with evidence from the text.

TThe brothers have separate rooms. Orsa is in Little Brothers bed and Little brother is the only one who finds her.

4. What did Orsa do at the end of the story? Support your answer with evidence from the text.

Orsa goes into another home, this time its a hive that belongs to bees.

Directions: Answer the following question by going back into the book.

1. Why did the Three Brothers go for a bike ride?

The Three brothers went for a bike ride to pass the time until their oatmeal cooled off.

2. How did Older brother respond when Middle Brother said his oatmeal was too hot?

Older Brother was kind and said he did not mean to make the oatmeal hot.

3. What is the lesson in the story?

The lesson in the story is to always lock your doors before going out and/or to not go into strangers homes.

Levels2Learning.com

Correlated to Current State Standards

www.ingramcontent.com/pod-product-compliance
Ingram Content Group UK Ltd.
Pitfield, Milton Keynes, MK11 3LW, UK
UKHW062001290726
14090UKWH00021B/1325